First, I want to give glory to God, from which all priceless blessings in life spawn. This book is dedicated to The Most High and my children. All have been instrumental in my growth. This book represents the heads up from an elder I wish I had. When you know the warning signs you have a fair chance in life. Not to say you won't fall...we all do. It's just that sometimes traps are set and children are not always aware. Kids entering into middle school and high school are right around the corner from adulthood. Many times children from urban environments are subject to the unnatural for so long that they begin to embrace it as reality. For instance, if someone is born into an abusive household, they may begin to feel pain is love. This book is a youth mentor in a manuscript.

Woman's Essence

Woman....who knocked you

from grace?

Who made you feel your

beauty wasn't innate?

Who made you feel you need

sexy clothes and a pose to

accentuate?

The essence of your aura glows

the brightest of hues

Woman you are

special..through you new life

blooms

Without you civilization is

doomed

Nothing on earth quite as

sacred as your womb

Rebuke lies, your spirit shines

you're divine beyond

opticals...

It's better to be yourself minus

enhancements...and feeling you

need to sell yourself for

advancements...

Woman you're a gift that's God

given

Real men know it's our duty to

love, honor and protect our

women...and children

Let's unify and start building

Mind Melting

Music used as a campaign to

brain mame

TV and radio's aim, ignorance

spray truth for the youth slayed

Music no longer represents

who we are...it reflects who

they want us to be

The reason it doesn't add up,

the math is corrupt

Media projects propaganda so

fan will lust cancerous

Rappers act as computers to

damage futures

It's a shame kids know Gucci

Mane not Mansa Musa.

Praising cancer tutors, amazing

how the outlandish maneuver

Face and name of wasted fad

craved over brave rulers

Who didn't purchase their

crown to astound from jewelers

Music industry ran off scams

by vultures

Emotional roller coasters from

sofas no visions of

sankofa..frequency scan,

media man molders

There are kids starving no

one's offering businesses

All the while we concurred thru

carcasses

 Kids fatherless retract maps to

consciousness

False kings reign over a pained

kingdom...plagues keep them

From speaking or retrieving

gems (wisdom)

Evil seeded thru demon

hymns..weak acceptance seek

thru stems (clothing)

seek to cleanse world seen with

a deeper lense

seeing sense depleted sins to

seek amends

Popularity of Pain

Why is pain and degradation

celebrated??

Many rappers nowadays are

utilized like dancing sambo to

justify our enslavement....

new wave minstrel movement

is perpetuated to condone our

blood stains on the

pavement....we parade this???

Broken souls...we find wealth

in our wounds...why???

Cried for so long from being

euthanized, the tube turns truth

to lies…

Engaging in our own genocide

with pride....why??

The unnatural is now

natural...fictions the new

factual…

When asked to get a grasp of

truth, it's a hassle to you?

You'd rather follow the map of

an active fool?

This system has castrated a

mass of youth…

Little to no proactive dad's,

heart prolapse stag (single male

with his heart in the wrong

place) alas path is bad…

Tragic cast into a magic mask

(embracing a false reality)

Where bags from the past are

hidden (hiding faults)

Precision passed to our

children…...

Animal

The goal is if you get a people

to take on animal

characteristics...look and act

like animals...who will feel

sorry for an animal that loses

its life? You're born

beautiful...a blessing from the

womb that grew....but life at

some point makes a born

blessing go into regression,

losing sight of their

essence....in evil's presence

turmoil sets in...depression that

can only be escaped thru drug

sessions...stifled some become

overgrown adolescents…

Animal...trapped in a realm

overwhelmed and feeling true

love is intangible..

War On Drugs

The moment you realize the

war on drugs was waged by the

same ones who put them there

in the first place. The same

ones who own private prisons

run the urban music division.

The music is senseless, a bunch

of commercials promoting bad

decisions...Guns, drugs and

alcohol sippin in our village

religious…

Gift about exquisite as

smallpox to men, women and

children...

Fetty climb (money grows)

from petty crime and

hatred..ignorance increases

defeated by sleeping agents .

same blankets given to natives

of this nation/corporation. The

reason some can't comprehend

what i am saying is because

they've been sedated.

Brain will evade any and all

knowledge penetration..mass

incarceration and death due to

your occupation...the thing is

this....

devils do favors for Needful

Things…

get all you ever wished for

praising the evil king…

you signed on the line didn't

even blink…

or take time to think, at some

point he will come to claim

your soul....is your life's value

priced in riches and gold?

Devil's lane cold you can't win

the game is fixed

..soured core, no more

motherless and fatherless

kids...plagued by generations of

post traumatic stress. In all this

God hasn't been mentioned

yet.they seek convictions and

breed division we seen as

threats ..you've been

conditioned to believe your

soul's existence is equated in

worldly checks...you have been

lied to....realize the tv is

designed to keep you blind

fools..remove the bind and get

mind food....no one is perfect

and I will never claim to

be...but lifes much better when

you can see....the worlds

greatest gifts are God given and

free....children, true love,

genuine friends and loyalty

Stolen Gems

Taking a man's greatness and

placed on a plantations

Divided & misguided the fam

and that man's hatred

Scrap can in famine that man

ate it Hard to fathom that plan

would expand ages

Shackles erase it debt at ya

neck replace it still segregated

Now who better at banking

measures is rated

Some excel when felons in

cells it's all business

Think where you dwell is better

than hell you're all senseless

Petroleum is liquid opium

liquor bought & sold in

emporiums

Now we all slaves to the

consortium

Shorties (children) still shine

though they're planted in bad

soil

Tribal Survival

Before our people were

Americanized we moved as a

tribe....but over time our truth

became minimized and was

penetrated by lies devised for

our demise...no guide, elder &

youth divide

Chains Remain

We all have been lied to...in a

sense well trained because

truthfully chains on the brain

still remain. We defy nature

and the natural order of things

on a daily basis.....paper

chasing endlessly but what

about the family structure....we

engage in mental and spiritual

masterbation instead of

rebuilding the nation....with the

media stations there's no need

for conventional plantations or

camps for

concentration....putrid pastors

vomit hatred and daily we've

all congregated.

Dazed Confused

No 40 acres....no mule....just

given a slew of tools to keep us

dazed and confused..brain

frame of a slave still in

tune..our ancestors would be

ashamed, we're

amused...staring at tubes in

amazement of coons...who act

like buffoons so their stocks

can balloon....let me ask

you...why is it cool to guzzle 40

oz of booze yet it's not cool to

spew jewelz....they're

encouraging you to consume

junk food instead of

nourishment ...cause they'd

rather see us killed or still

instead of flourishing

Trends

A trend that teaches value

vanity over humanity

I guess because you're a fan of

brands you're more of a man

than me

Insanity living a fantasy people

pose

What's important, true soul or

your shoe soles?

Fact, souls and soles grow old

Either designs you consume or

defined by you

I'm talking true glows over

fool's gold

Over harsh roads travel

decayed

Adolescent stage plague, never

unraveled with age

Appearance vs spirit &

adherence to GOD

Gift vs an exquisite mirage of

living large

In actually it;s all a facade or

ego massage

Camouflage, A way to mentally

dodge some of your

shortcomings

For those who floss false & lost

fronting, your karma of course

coming

Black Babies

The minds of the black babies

are under attack...and no one

sees it because nowadays lies

are disguised as fact.

Look at what's promoted to

them constantly in their tv

stations…

Oversexualization, taught that

there's no beauty in their

natural pigmentation, taught

that their God given hair

texture in society is

unappreciated

Kids ushered into an alternate

brain pattern.

Nothing matters...it's ok that tv

depicts women going from

harlot to starlet. Nowadays a

farce where the heart is. Life's

a game of charades, resume

ingrained into parchment...all

for a flash car and some

garments. In darkness,

hardened and disheartened

soul of a slave who crave

knowledge. School of hard

knocks replace college for

those whose wallets just are not

brolic. Due to our realm, lost

sight of ourselves

Nothing matters...anything goes now....everyone deserves respect even if they have no respect for themselves..everyone else's rights and reparations supersede ours...and why?? The answer is simple...they have standards… If Native Americans see their culture being depicted in a foul manner they ban together and get it shut down...or they won't support it. We have been conditioned to love our own degradation....this is madness and no one cares.... I'm the one who is tripping. Some of these adults may be lost forever...but at least

save the children....

Vein Pain

I'm in pain...cause seems we're

all in struggle to

gain...spiritually slain, now

only a soulless vessel

remains..Yes it is a new year

but that doesn't exclude the

rules to adhere...and to me they

appear very clear...people

trying to treat codes of conduct

like puff daddy in the

90s...concoct mad remixes..

take heed and listen....

Evil depictions of splendid

spiritual lynchings

Living bad is a drag & Bags

passed to the children

Lad or a las depleted seeking

conviction

Vixens dismissed for depictions

of classy women

No more glimpses henchmen or

dad's in prison

Souls no longer thrashed during

mass division

Sleepless Man

Can't sleep..up feeling old and

sad...thinking it's a shame that

we live in world driven by fad..

whatever's trending controls

where we're spending our cash.

Enslaved, we pay crazy

amounts for powerball...but

stall when a selfless donations

involved...A pure of heart

donation...one that's not blasted

on the radio or tv

station...giving from the heart

minus the social media farce.

Why do we allow fads to shape

our moves?

Falling in line like cattle when

bells are rattled. Why can't we

do things from the heart? Daily

we all log on for a fix....in life

now this is as real as it gets....it

pains my soul....

I feel sad and old, from seeing

another cash stack pose,

another woman's back that's

shown all flash and no abstract

notes. Left wondering who

they're minus a mask…

It's grade school extended ...to

be liked, people **will** travel

endless....

How can one be deeply rooted

if the soil is being polluted?

Clueless we've all been suited

for nooses....brothers and

sisters battle for what the truth

is…

People dismiss GOD and truth

for fiction that man gives them.

Everyone's ambition is a

chance to enhance glisten...

I talk, yet walk in contradiction,

guess in some ways we're all

lost in a false religion..

We praise those with man-

made fame religiously…

Log for a fogged lense and

clogged sense religiously.

Work hard till our souls worn

so digits seen….. Religiously..

Not judging others this my own

moment of reflection…

Imagine the world if we

worked together ...none of us

are perfect...none of us are

worthless...we all fall...live and

learn..no one man or woman

greater than another..when

stripped of all you own....what's

left?

Erase the profile pics....what

are we left with? The soul of a

person reflects who they truly

are....everything else a

distraction from where the fact

is.

Breath of Life

Glory to The Most High for awakening me this morning. While I have the breath of life, I always have another chance to do right. Understand that God can provide light in a dim lit life. No man nor woman made object can offer anything greater...! will not live my days in fear of cops or my peers...the God to which I adhere has a message that's clear....everything else is a fog aimed to misguide how life is steered....all isn't as it appears.

Faith

So wait, let me get this

straight....you don't believe in

God, yet you believe in on

screen facades?? Media

dictates your talk.walk and

thought....so I guess the Tube is

your God.....think about it.

most either embracing a

mirage or chasing mental

massage...digital

frauds...visuals God given a

lost mission, embark on

ritualistic tune ins...praise

given..soul as a whole

imprisoned..though a compass

enclosed, genuine scrolls

missing...what's on your dome?

I chose distance from

clones...GPS phone target by

drones..beats for a feces thesis

cologne..hate container,

plagued by anger...no favorite

athletes or

entertainers .. nor do I adore

slave labor to hoard

paper..bills extort for escort

favors..Hopeless, the focus is

follow and be followed..one

becomes hollow, boast swine

no design for tomorrow.

Focus

Where is your daily focus

devoted??? The world is where

it's at because we have become

consumed with everything but

acknowledging and following

God...7 days in a week...some

engage in nonsense for six and

give praise one day for a

couple of hours....99%of the

time your soul is being

devoured....give praise and

acknowledgment daily to The

Most High...this is laid out

plain and simple...How can you

love God but only devote one

day and a hour to praise??

Honor your mother and father,

respect your origin, without it

you wouldn't be here. In a

unified relationship, how can

you love someone without

acknowledging them...daily?

We all including myself are self

centered that's ultimately why

we are hindered...human

bonsai trees...beautiful yet

stifled from growing to our full

potential.

Young Men

Young men

beware...understand that they

either want you...emasculated,

incarcerated or

incapacitated...all three

instances are a form of

castration. Find a quality wife

and build a quality life. Raise

your children without struggle

or strife

Men the community needs you

to protect it again

Young man be a soldier for the

right cause never bend

Young men without you

maintaining a clear lense, bad

cycles can never end

Look up how lions move...they

roam in family packs, be the

replica

Of a king that protects his

Queen and seeds from

predators.

It's easier to follow leads than

blaze your own trail

We only live once, so why do it

in the shadow of another male

Not saying you can not build

with your brother, but establish

your own throne

Something that you can leave

to your children when you are

gone.

Being a man is not about cash,

flash and a bunch of women

Being a man is being brave

enough to make a dark world

different

No if you can't beat them join

them mentality

The battle against demons is

life long, to join is a fatality

Young black man, we have

seen enough casualties

Young black man you are

special..again the duty is to

protect not to disrespect our

women

Young man, between vixen and

genuine women, there is a

difference

Quality over quantity

responsibility over indifference

Be wise with decisions because

a seed planted today is a

harvest reaped tomorrow

So be conscious not to sow

seeds of pain and sorrow

I know society molds wants

you cold and hollow

God or man...there is only one

you can follow

make it a trend to be genuine

men again

Franz Mesmer

Minds designed to follow

behind movements but blind to

align where the true is.....

Stop having pride in

movements designed to

enslave, degrade and eliminate

you...following what's trending

doesn't mean you're

winning....just means you're

good at falling in and

pretending... Seeing someone

go astray and helping them

correct their ways isn't a

diss...we have to love & uplift

Savagery

Brothers frightened for their

life when sirens & lights

around

Moment of silence for Mike

Brown,

Lost his life for a night on the

town

In their iris we're all tyrants

silenced by pounds

Canine style, cave lifestyle no

hard sentencing

Cowards in power by thin veils

derail villages

The game plagued by stale

lyricists

Bank statements raising for

satan's apprentices

Soul apprehended for

benjamins (money), you all

simpletons to them

No longer civilians, reptilian

citizen system set for killing the

citizen since genesis

Black Dollars

End of enslavement happened

for trapping the black dollar

Mental lynch rituals is essential

for black squalor

Family life no longer attractive

to black fathers

To prevail harder in a prison

cell or martyred

No wonder there's a lack of

black scholars

Til we're subtracting the black

collars shackled knowledge

God's people need to gather

and toss evil

Beyond holocaust all of our

loss equal

Lost thugs, sports, drugs,

entertainment, toss slugs,

thoughts slumped minus

arraignment Detain men

insane blood staining the

pavement by days end

War-like maze we raised in

face hunger

Either Dekkard (human) or

Battie (android) in Blade

Runner (film with human vs

robot. Basically you can either

be human or emotionless as an

android in the game of life)

Ethnically cleansed in need of a

lense badly

Prison and no daddy turn men

batty

Feminine face buried in nappy

happy look

Yet how God made Eve and

Adam the baddest book?

My last draft scrapped it new

word mapped it

Syran madness, saddened by

savage police tactics

Nina…

Most thugs are rarely like Nas

in Belly

Fans grabbing a cot if you jot

heavily

Drug spots, plot for the cops let

it be

Roofs in need of repair to bare

climate

Before you're impaired by it,

cheer violence, weird science

Get silenced for eyeing change,

iron bang till you realize it like

"I'm in chains"

Brain frame of a slave

narrative, straight characters

These chains karatless ancestral

embarrassment

Barring kids, led to die but born

to live, exploring gifts

Orator through overtures

holding the fist

Worlds frozen no one scolding

the kids

Within hopelessness sit, no one

scoping for sense

Just clothing and hoping to

rope in some sense off a opiate

lit

Facade Squad
Lying on camera in America to
camouflage tombs,
Music industry fog move, odd

cool cattle prod fathering loss

moves

Full on fools, gun armed goons

cancerous like a pull on kools

or Newport

Rap tunes is Lucifer new sport

Shame what dudes will do for a

new fort, it's cool as long as

their food forked (selling the

soul for worldly gain has been

popularized in a genre that was

once about unity and

education)

Ashes 2 Childhood

City is gentrified by insidious

sinful guys

Behind riches the hideous hide

oblivion rise to oblivious eyes

Get a glimpse at the

time..commission decisions out

of citizens sight so division will

rise

Senseless with crime,

sentenced to time, kids living a

lie

Blemishes bind hid in his mind

is a dark feeling from hard

living

They're born scorned with no

amore given

Thirsting for whores and

Porsche wheeling galore

killings

Rappers distort children who

can't afford building

Course feelings from all the

lost morgue victims

Villains still in the village

living with faults in them

Mass killings eugenics and

drug chemists thug kinsmen

Young henchmen who's lovin'

to mug women

cuff sentence because they're

lusting for plush living

In ghetto prisons they guinea

pig children

Chasing a rap image cap

peeling gat (gun) wielding

For stacks (money) off crack

dealing

American dream money

machine suffer & bleed

Still enslave seeds who crave

cheese

Mistakes lead to grave or a

cage seen for wage needs

Feel you're tall but your small

scale

Path cost fall with no guard rail

Harsh tale of innocence lost

Citizens forced to endure

ignorance tossed within their

midst

Once fond the bond has gone

sense

When the cameras on

click...behind it all switch

Most flawed, beauty facade like

Shamaylan flicks

God's Children…...Awaken
Children of God so we're

persecuted

Every person on earth polluted

purse pursuing

Purge the cooning in music no

substance to it

Urchin lurk with nooses

ruthless public executions

For viewing, stomach ruin like

culture when vultures flew in

Heart trashed, sheep

slaughtered by false flags

To God ask, why Tulsa (Black

Wall Street Massacre) got

bomb crashed, and no one's

alarmed by the harm cast

Nothing's evolved its all fact

compiled, sadly

Seen our green mile since the

Nile valley

Wowed then ask me

information upon indication of

my indignation

Of the administration

facilitating the situation

Reformation, Reparations

beyond monetarily we need

solidarity

Listen carefully, can't expect

others to care for we

End black genocide.

Snatched from Africa into the

American rapture

Mind massacre even after

stained brain matter

Lives shattered uncommon

disaster years battered

Had our vision tattered by

villains amidst lies

Wigs fried hard to win in a

fixed time

Uplift blind, mind design

slavery refined

From the field tensions to

prison confines (13th

Amendment)

Scribe sense and cleanse a

condensed mind

Live in times where the dense

shine and make clout

Pay you for brain droughts no

escape route

Amazed how it's either sell out

or braille for bail outs

Meaning you're blind

intentionally or un-willingly

Shun imagery, stunned by the

sun's energy

Visual of the spiritual vampire

chemistry

Untie eye binds...sublime mind

Regardless of the barricades
society makes...realize who you
are...all children are a gift from
above...so carry yourself as
such. Respect others as you
would have them respect you.
Worldly wealth does not reflect
your worth. Also do not be
afraid to be unique...always be
yourself. Be brave and
confident...have faith that your
dreams can be achieved. This
book is dedicated to the leaders
of tomorrow. Our time on this
earth is limited, so use your
time wisely. The people you

hang around have a huge effect on your life. Surround yourself with positive people that want to do good in the world. The world needs more innovators and less imitators. No matter where you are from, you can make it. Turn the tv off and read about unsung heroes from the past. Read about the obstacles they had to overcome before they made history. Love, patience, honesty, respect and happiness….be defined by those things.

WE all begin from our
father's seed planted in
our mother's womb,
which is soil. In our
lives we have to endure
all types of weather,
same as all plant life.
Gardens that are tended
to usually flourish. We
are all flowers...we can
either choose to blossom
beautifully or wilt and
wither. This book is
simply about how
various elements will try
to get into your soil and

ruin your growth. Can

you imagine if a rose

had a brain? Would a

rose know its purpose?

Would a rose allow

poison to saturate its

soil? Would a rose

surround itself with

weeds that impede on its

growth? Meaning if

something you partake

in is not good for your

core, why engage? You

have a choice young

blessing…. Blossom….

Made in the USA
Middletown, DE
22 September 2017